stop hurting my friends!

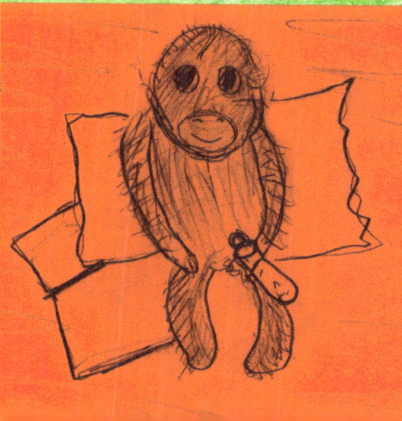

Foreword

One Special Orangutan is clearly a labor of love for all those involved. The book is special, not just because Budi the orangutan is special or because the species as a whole is special; this book is special as it conveys the threats to orangutans, such as deforestation and fires, as perceived by children. It also offers much hope from the children, who believe that rehabilitation of orangutans for future release and reducing consumer demands such as for palm oil can help protect the forests that the orangutans live in.

According to scientific publications and the media, the future of orangutans in Borneo and Sumatra is under much threat. Over the past 100 years, a lot of orangutan habitats in these regions have been lost to agriculture. The distribution of orangutans is now only at the more remote sites in these two islands.

Across Borneo and Sumatra, at least three different threats have been identified. The first is that the majestic forests in which orangutans live are constantly being logged and converted, and in some cases burned and replanted with plantation crops such as oil palms. In places where forests are burned, orangutans that cannot escape are sadly burned with their homes. Images of burnt orangutans that repeatedly appear in the media and conservation websites reveal the enormity of the problem as well as the cruelty associated with it.

The second threat is that some orangutans are hunted for consumption. Orangutans are seen as a protein source for these hunters, and their plight is not easily addressed as enforcement levels in these remote sites are low.

The third threat is that young orangutans are sometimes caught and sold into the pet trade. As no mum would gladly give her young away, the mother orangutans are often killed. If young orangutans are fortunate enough to be rescued, the difficult task of rehabilitating them for eventual release into the wild starts. Sadly, conservation of orangutans for release to the wild requires money. The contributions of the children of P.S. 107 from the proceeds of the sale of this book will help us pay for some of the costs incurred when trying to rehabilitate these orphans.

In this wonderful book, the children in P.S. 107 have been able to communicate the complexities of orangutan conservation in a manner that is remarkably easy to understand. Indeed, readers will be engaged from the very first word. It is my belief that people of all ages and backgrounds will enjoy the children's passionate and imaginative story-telling which brings alive images of this wonderful creature, the orangutan.

Congratulations to the students of P.S. 107.

Melvin T. Gumal
Wildlife Conservation Society Malaysia Program Director
Winner of the Whitley Award for Conservation in Ape Habitats 2014

Hi. My name
is Budi.

I'm a Bornean
orangutan.

Orangutan means "man of the forest."
Like chimpanzees, gorillas and bonobos, I'm a great ape.

I live in Indonesia, which is located near the equator and has a tropical climate.

We have a dry and a wet season. In the wet season, the rainforest blooms into life.

PACIFIC
OCEAN

Borneo

Sumatra

INDONESIA

INDIAN   OCEAN

There are about 250 million people here, many volcanoes, and more than 17,500 islands.

Orangutans live in just two places — the islands of Borneo and Sumatra.

We are the biggest tree-living animals in the world. We have flexible hips, long arms, and long hands and feet that can grip. We have hair on our whole body.

Right now I'm small, but I will grow up to be strong and tall.

Orangutans are climbing machines. We live in the tippy-top of trees, and build nests every night so we can sleep in them. We put big leaves on top of our nests like roofs, so when it rains, the water doesn't get us wet.

Sometimes we climb 120 feet up a tree at night just to build a nest. Now you tell me, are we amazing or what?

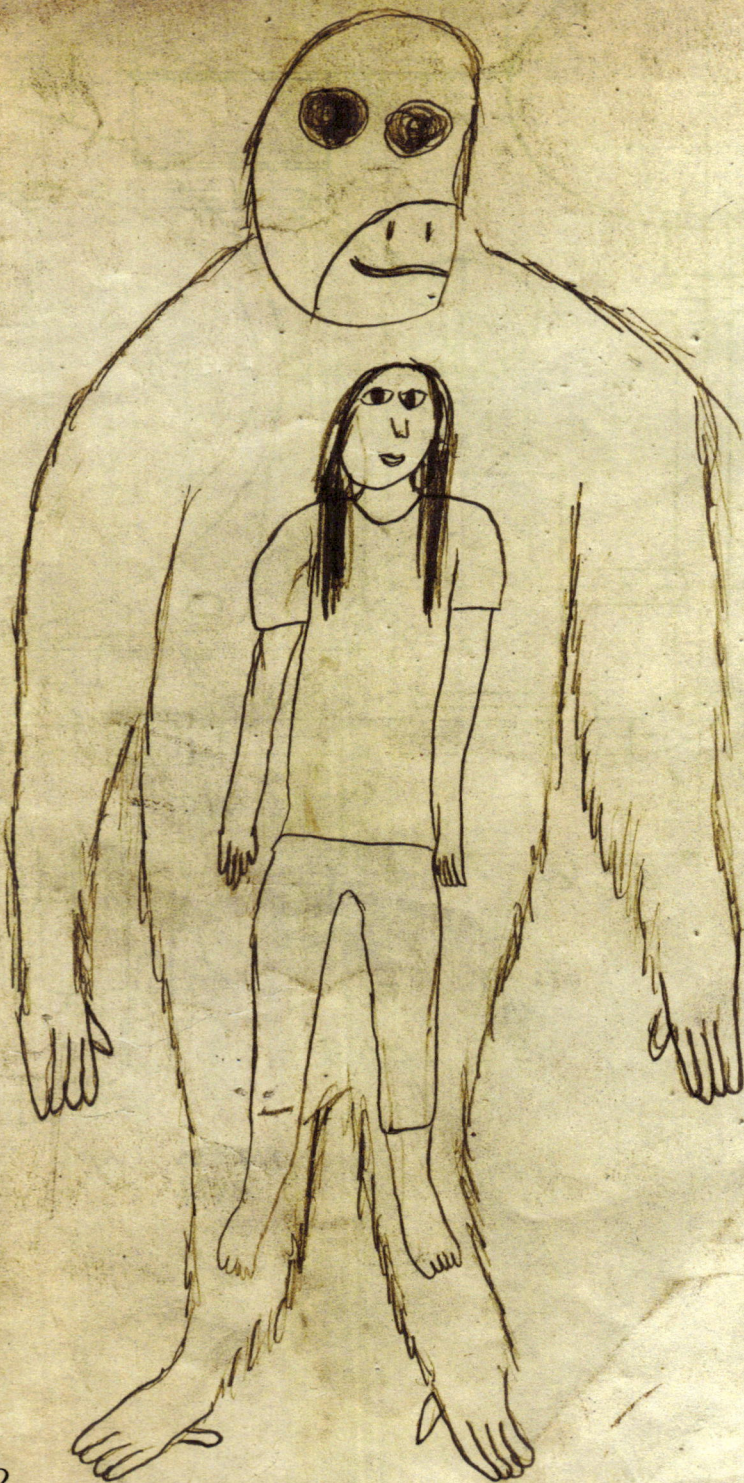

Humans and orangutans are very similar. We share 97 percent of the same DNA.

DNA is like a blueprint for you, your body, your habits, and your personality. This means that I am 97 percent you. You are 97 percent me. We're nearly relatives (though I am so much better looking than you)!

The sad thing is, my species is in danger. There are only 14,000 orangutans left in Sumatra, and between 45,000 to 70,000 of us in Borneo. We have lost more than half of our species in the last sixty years, because people are destroying our homes.

Every day, humans come and burn the jungles to plant palm trees. They turn the burned land into palm oil plantations.

You might think it's all right because the animals can come back and live there. But we can't, because the palm trees don't have food or shelter. And when they are planted, nothing else can grow there.

Indonesia was two-thirds covered in rain forests, but it's not anymore.

The forests are being destroyed. It happens a little each year, but you can see the damage that's being done. It's like watching hopes, dreams, and orangutan aspirations die.

Now what we have is sad animals, burned-down forests, and no place for orangutans to live.

Fire. That stuff is not just hot. It's more like a burning soul-taking that comes after you until you are gone.

It's not just harming us. It's also hurting other species of animals, including you.

The fires have created a toxic smog that is surrounding Indonesia. And the burning also lets out a kind of gas called methane, which causes global warming.

My forest used to be big and bright. There were fresh green leaves and pretty, colorful flowers in shades of orange, red, yellow, purple, blue, and pink.

There were lots of streams and wet patches in the forest. Most of the time it was hot, but the rain cooled us down.

I had a lot of neighbors. There were tigers, lizards, and bandicoots, as well as other orangutans. I learned to stay away from the ferocious komodo dragons. And I wasn't exactly friendly with those crocodiles.

But some were nice, like the birds.

My mom and I had tall trees to nest in and swing from, and lots of food. We ate bark, leaves, flowers, a variety of bugs, over 300 different kinds of fruit, and 500 different plants. Yum!

We would sit on the trees and watch the sun fall out of the sky and the moon replace it.

We had so much fun.

Then one day, I smelled smoke. It hurt my lungs. The air grew even hotter than normal. Then I saw humans. They were burning my home.

My mom grabbed me and started running as fast as she could to get away. I couldn't see, and breathing was hard. All around me, the forest was disappearing fast.

I quickly turned my head and saw it all — my home, happiness, and family — just burning to the ground. Then I was all alone.

Big hands picked me up. Human hands. I wriggled but couldn't get away. Then the humans chained me to metal. I felt sleep drift over me.

The men took me away and carried me to the village. They sold me to a lady who stuffed me in a chicken cage and kept me as a pet. There was little space to move, and only a blanket and a squeaky toy.

I started to cry for my mama. I was just two months old.

Days went by. I was never let out of the cage and never fed anything but condensed milk, day and night. The stuff made me feel horrible.

I was dying slowly, a little bit each day. My limbs were swollen and bent, my body bloated. I even lost my furry, award-winning hair. It was scary, and my tummy hurt.

I hoped for a day when this would stop, and eventually the day came.

23

When the door to my cage opened, I shivered from cold and fear. But the humans I saw were not my owner. They had worried eyes and picked me up gently and took me out of my small chicken cage.

What's happening? I was very confused.

Soon I heard the rustle of wheels. They loaded me on a van.

After a long time, we arrived at a collection of buildings in the middle of a forest. A sign said IAR – International Animal Rescue.

When I got there, more people were waiting. I cried when they picked me up. I didn't understand they were helping.

The International Animal Rescue helps orangutans like me survive. The sanctuary purchased 300 acres of land for something called a "rehabilitation facility," a nice big place that could house one hundred orangutans.

They help reeducate us so one day we can go out on our own and live in the forest like an orangutan should.

When I first got to the sanctuary, I had to pass a lot of health tests.
I got a lot of shots. They really hurt.

My new cage was much more comfortable than the chicken one.
It was not dirty or dark, clammy or cold. I felt like I could relax in it,
if I wasn't hurting so much.

I yelped as the humans touched me. I felt scared, tight, and sick. I was being lifted from a comfortable bed and put down on a cold metal surface.

Soon, one of them started pressing a bottle to my lips. I didn't even have the strength to open my mouth. The milk they fed me was yummy, not thick and sweet like the milk I'd had before. But eating takes so much energy, I could only have a few small sips.

My caretakers wear masks to protect us, the orangutans, from getting human diseases.

Finally, their strange faces grew familiar.

I really love my veterinarian, Dr. Karmele Llano Sanchez. She knew how I felt, how much pain I was in. She was almost like a second mom.

Ow! Stop! that hurts! woagh!

My new friends take care of me.

A doctor named Ayu helps me walk again. My legs are still very weak, but it's a great improvement to my "beaten-up" self, when I would cry out in pain just from sitting up.

I can finally lift my own milk bottle to drink. I tasted sweet delicious fruit for the first time.

They take me in a big red wheelbarrow over to "baby school," where baby orangutans learn all the things our moms would have taught us: how to climb, what to eat and what not to eat, how to live and care for ourselves in the wild. We swing on trees and climb to platforms. We love to play in sawdust, just like you like to play in sand!

Afterwards, I'm very tired. Who knew playing was such hard work!

When I first started baby school, I clung to my best friend, Jemmi. He was the youngest orangutan ever to come here.

He was kept as a pet too. A rescue team found him tied up in a box outside his owner's home. He had a rash from the rope and he was dehydrated.

He was only four months old.

Meeting Jemmi was one of the happiest days of my life.

At first, I was a bit shy. But soon enough we were climbing and playing in the hammock. Sharing it makes me feel so welcome and safe.

I am much happier with Jemmi by my side at the rescue center. He pushes me to work hard and helps me when I'm down.

He and I have a secret. We both lost our mothers.

Sometimes I lie in bed and wonder what happened to her.

I wish I could touch her, feel her warm hands. Climb with her. Do everything I do in the sanctuary, but with her.

At night, I dream about her as the best orangutan in the world.

Now I can jump, swing, eat and play, just like an orangutan is supposed to. When I finish baby school, I'm moving up to forest school.

That's where we'll climb higher trees and build nests to sleep in, and if we're ready, we can even spend the night in the nest.

It's the last step before being on our own. Some of my friends are excited about that, because it's like being a real orangutan.

But even with the help of all the volunteers, some of us won't make it back to the wild.

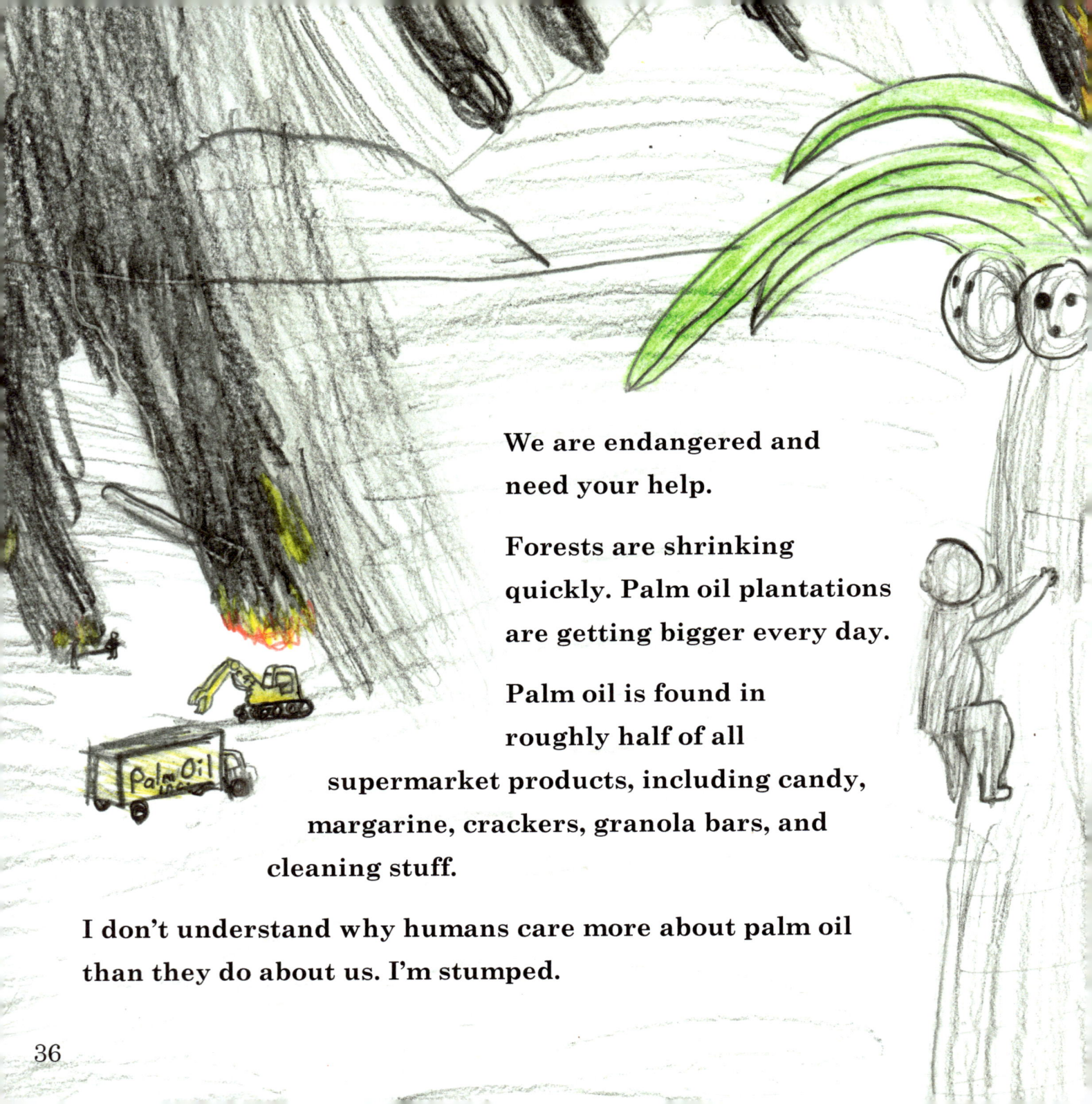

We are endangered and need your help.

Forests are shrinking quickly. Palm oil plantations are getting bigger every day.

Palm oil is found in roughly half of all supermarket products, including candy, margarine, crackers, granola bars, and cleaning stuff.

I don't understand why humans care more about palm oil than they do about us. I'm stumped.

If deforestation keeps going like this, there will be hardly any trees left for orangutans like me. If orangutans become extinct, it means that there will be a world without us — no other orangutans and no me.

But you can help. Boycott groceries that contain palm oil. Tell all your friends and family about it. You can also donate to International Animal Rescue, the organization that rescued me.

Don't go and try to buy an orangutan. That can't end well.

Here, the forest is clean and bright, like the one I remembered with my mother. The trees are tall and overflowing with green. The air is warm and moist, but not too hot. Very different from the burning mess I left more than a year ago.

I climb up the tree, breathing up nature's smell. I only have to climb a little to see the big, never-ending blue sky!

I used to have nightmares, but now I dream that I will climb high into the treetops.

I see a future of green and life and forests. I see a life with little or no palm oil. I see a world where peace and happiness overcome greed.

I hope there will be more orangutans, swinging through the trees.

Afterword

I firmly believe that the only way to build a better future for animals is to educate the young of today. You can imagine therefore just how delighted I was to read this beautiful book written and illustrated by the fifth graders of P.S. 107 John W. Kimball Learning Center.

The students quite clearly have an excellent grasp of the problems facing Indonesia's dwindling rainforests. Moreover, the fact that they were able to relate to and be moved by Budi's plight has strengthened my belief in the importance and the relevance of our work for everyone, young and old, who cares about the natural environment and its wildlife.

The illustrations are delightful and at the same time a little sinister. They portray perfectly the pressure and the threats to the orangutan's survival in our modern world.

The human drive to make maximum profit by exploiting every inch of rainforest for the production of palm oil comes at an extremely heavy price. Such widespread deforestation is taking a tragic toll on all living things. It is decimating wildlife habitats and leaving orangutans without food, shelter, or protection from hunters.

International Animal Rescue's team in West Borneo reaches out to rural communities who are likely to encounter orangutans that are forced into villages and onto farmland in search of food. The team explains that the presence of orangutans is not a sign that their numbers are plentiful but rather an indication that their forest home is shrinking. When they learn that orangutans are endangered and face huge threats to their survival, most people are willing to help protect, rather than persecute them. This is a huge step in the right direction.

My hope is that the children of Borneo will grow up with a determination to protect and preserve their natural environment and the wildlife that inhabits it. By carrying out sustainable harvesting of palm oil as a natural resource, but also setting aside areas of rainforest for wildlife, palm oil companies and other agro-industries in Indonesia can bring a halt to the decline of orangutan populations and make a vital difference to orangutan conservation.

The fact that Budi's story has inspired the creation of such a wonderful book gives me real confidence for the future. It proves that our message is being heard and heeded by those who matter most. With the help of young people like the authors of *One Special Orangutan* I do believe the orangutan can survive in the wild for generations to come.

Alan Knight OBE
CEO, International Animal Rescue

Acknowledgements

The PS 107 Beast Relief committee would like to thank the following individuals and organizations for their support.

The International Animal Rescue (IAR) provided essential guidance, an introduction to the orangutans of Borneo and Sumatra and the story of Budi himself. We are grateful to Alan Knight, Chief Executive Officer, for contributing an afterword. Sophie Pollmann and Lis Key generously supplied research materials, photographs, and their expertise. The heroic IAR staff in Indonesia, including Karmele Llano Sanchez and Ayu Budi Handayani, have saved and improved the lives of many orangutans.

The Arcus Foundation offered advice and helped launch this project, by connecting Beast Relief with IAR. At Arcus, we are indebted to Great Apes team members Annette Lanjouw and Linda May, as well as Ericka Novotny and Bryan Simmons for their guidance.

Special thanks to Melvin T. Gumal, director of the Wildlife Conservation Society's Malaysia Program and a 2014 Whitley conservation award winner, who contributed a foreword.

Eve Litwack, P.S. 107's principal, encouraged this project and provided essential logistical support. Fifth-grade teachers Michael Carlson, Ed Schulz, and Shirley Harkins helped bring this project to all 87 fifth graders. And of course, without our talented fifth graders, there would be no book. All the illustrations and words in this book are their own.

Beast Relief also acknowledges its book committee in bringing this project to fruition. Members include: Julie Brunner Cross, Katherine Eban, Mary Huhn, Maureen McLaughlin, Heather Millward, Ericka Novotny, Grace Sharfstein, and Tracy Tullis.

Emma Safira Mikayla
Rebecca Katherine
Luby Christian Cynthia
Leo Graham Soren Angelo
Isabel Clara Safia Brandon
Fernando Lycianne Trevor
Patrick Gigi Rachael William
Samara Rory Maeve Ava Jacob
Auden Ella Miles Emily Sonja
Taina Erika Leila Ina Ela
Mina Talia Katherine Sam
Johnny Matthew
Nicholas Luli Matt Nicholas Romi
Kylee James Gabriella
Imre Isaac Cody Thaddeus
Fiona Ana Hugo Aurora Cathrine
Lucie Maya Owen Leila Rose
Taya Rory Harper Sophia Killian
Katie Mila Henry Jonah Caroline
Sarah Lucia Arthur Jesse

Sonja
Bella
Chloe
Aiden
Derek
Charles
Cassius
Cristyana

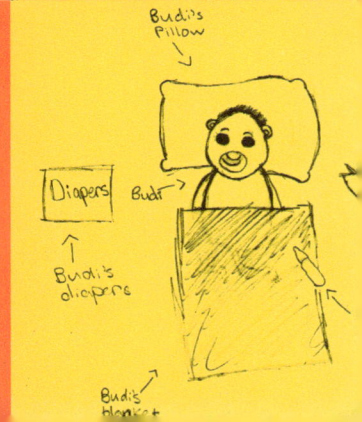

www.ingramcontent.com/pod-product-compliance
Lightning Source LLC
Chambersburg PA
CBHW042055040426

42447CB00003B/240